the messy
MIDDLE

*Encouraging you through the frustrating gap between
where you are now and where you want to be*

Stephanie O'Brien-Martin

NEW YORK

LONDON • NASHVILLE • MELBOURNE • VANCOUVER

the messy MIDDLE

© 2018 Stephanie O'Brien-Martin

Published in New York, New York, by Morgan James Publishing. Morgan James is a trademark of Morgan James, LLC.
www.MorganJamesPublishing.com

The Morgan James Speakers Group can bring authors to your live event. For more information or to book an event visit The Morgan James Speakers Group at www.TheMorganJamesSpeakersGroup.com.

ISBN 978-1-68350-583-9 paperback
ISBN 978-1-68350-584-6 eBook
Library of Congress Control Number: 2017907495

Cover & Interior Design by:
Megan Whitney
Creative Ninja Designs
megan@creativeninjadesigns.com

In an effort to support local communities, raise awareness and funds, Morgan James Publishing donates a percentage of all book sales for the life of each book to Habitat for Humanity Peninsula and Greater Williamsburg.

Get involved today! Visit
www.MorganJamesBuilds.com

This book is credited to the one who inspired, taught, directed, and refined me through the process of my own Messy Middle: my Lord and Savior Jesus Christ. Without your Holy Spirit, I never would have made it through.

This book is dedicated to the love of my life, best friend, and husband: Christopher Martin. You refused to allow me to give up through the Messy Middle though many times I threatened it. Your belief in and support of my dream and purpose have allowed this book to become a reality.

table of
CONTENTS

GREETINGS!

Have you ever longed to be somewhere different than where you are? Have you always known deep down that you are meant to be much more than what you currently are? Perhaps you have a vision of what you think your life should look like but have no idea how to make it come to pass. Do you have a sense of what you are here to contribute but have no clarity or focus regarding how to achieve it?

In my last year of college, I had a dream of doing great work, similar to someone like Joel Osteen or Dave Ramsey—though I did not want to actually be a pastor or financial advisor. I wanted to write books and help inspire others to have the beautiful lives they longed to live. People would ask me what I was going to write about. I had no idea, but that didn't stop me from looking for direction.

To make that dream happen, I chose the profession of social work with the intention of later getting my master's degree and becoming a counselor. I thought that my work would inspire me, and that the contents of this book would just come to me.

But less than two years into my first job out of college, I was very discontent in my job. I was angry and confused because I had been so sure that social work was what I always wanted to do. I was certain I would love that career. Instead, I felt stuck, overwhelmed, and trapped in a line of work I had no passion for. I felt like it robbed me of joy, energy, and life.

I prayed for guidance and revelation for what my new job would be and what my next step was. I still had a strong desire to write a book, and every year that I got closer to thirty years old, that desire grew stronger.

My prayers did not go unanswered—in fact, God immediately began showing me the answer to my prayers and began guiding me. Yet, I was blocked from hearing, seeing, trusting, and believing, because to truly follow His will for my life, I had to let go of something that was very important to me at the time, something that I idolized and used as my security. I had a personal situation in my life that kept me from trusting God and walking in my purpose. As soon as I let go of that, my life radically changed for the better.

Six months before beginning to write this book, I started my own business as a career and life coach. Before I started my business, God led me to the 48 Days Coaching With Excellence seminar. I had no idea why I needed to go, but I followed His guidance. After that conference, I came home and immediately started working on my business. Now, I am slowly but steadily building and growing my coaching business. It's been quite a ride.

I had assumed that once my purpose was revealed to me, it would be smooth sailing. Doors would easily open and I would walk in an abundance of favor. I believed that I would immediately reach the levels of success I envisioned. Little did I know that much time, many lessons, and a lot of hard work are involved in seeing one's vision come to fruition.

In this book you will find some stories of people who uncovered their purpose, and the journey they went through to see their dreams come alive. You will also find the path that many successful people have taken through the difficult times. This is a book about transformation and transition. It will serve as encouragement, inspiration, and practical how-to guidance of how to truly let go of the old and receive the new to live the life that Christ died for us to have.

an unexpected
SURPRISE

In J.R.R. Tolkien's *The Hobbit*, we read about a character who had a comfortable life, but who was brought from that state of being into a better life. Bilbo Baggins was a rather content character, and as far as his outlook on life was concerned, everything was idyllic. He did not want any adventures, and the book narrates this sentiment very clearly in his meeting with Gandalf on one fine morning. His life didn't go the way he expected, however—to the benefit of many.

His nephew Frodo had a very different outlook on the matter of adventure, thanks in part to Bilbo's unexpected and unwelcomed adventure years before. Although he also was in love with his homeland, he longed for adventure and wanted to experience for himself something like what his adored uncle had experienced, and had recounted on numerous occasions.

Both Bilbo and Frodo ended up being on very astounding adventures. One wanted adventure; one did not. We can start by taking notice of this.

This book is not a success manual in what has become the traditional sense of the word. There are many such manuals in bookstores and on the Internet. Rather, it is an inside look at what I have come to understand as a hidden obstacle that gets in the way for many of us as we try to chart a path to whatever we consider "success" to be. As in the lives of the two Bagginses, our own lives take unexpected turns. We plan, but the results are often wildly different than those we planned for. What's more, the process and journey we take to try to achieve these goals we set *also* go awry, and in some strange and unpredictable ways.

What I hope to do here is to help the reader recognize this, and not be afraid of it. Success can come to any of us, but the way to achieve it is rarely the way we tell ourselves it will come. I want to talk about this process, especially the most difficult and trying parts of it, as a way to help to those who are trying to chart their path in life and to find joy in living here—and hereafter.

the great
BEGINNING

In the introduction, I told you about how I had some plans for my life that seemed very noble and exciting. I dreamed of the results of my great work, and just knew in my mind how wonderful everything would be. As I started to pursue my goal, the path looked bright, true, and actually, everything seemed easy enough at first. Challenges were "to be expected" but after all, I was going to achieve this Great Work, so a little trouble with a class or an assignment was no big deal. All the stories I knew about successful people had this common element: they had faced challenges and difficulties, but they never lost their way as they moved toward their greatness. Surely that would be my own experience.

Little did I know.

The logical course I took seemed to blow up in my face, and it was inexplicable. After all, hadn't I prayed for this? Wasn't I doing the right thing because I asked God for it and I was going for it with all my heart? I was, and yet nothing seemed to be working. In fact, forget "seemed." It *wasn't* working at all!

I later learned that this is actually much closer to reality for everyone than the story we are sold is to reality. The beginning of our pursuit of success often starts with a great bang and lots of joy as we rush forward to fulfill our destinies. But then things begin to happen. First there are "challenges" that seem easily surmountable. Then the really hard stuff comes, and the really hard stuff has stopped many people dead in their tracks. Why? Because they have been told that it is not supposed to be that way.

Most of us have a lot of determination and courage, so we take this in stride as best we can, but eventually doubt creeps in. And, usually, things continue to become more and more difficult. My desire to write a book kept getting stronger as I got older. But at the same time, I kept coming up with nothing to write about. I mean *nothing*. It had me bewildered, because *that was not the way it was supposed to be!*

As I finished school and began working professionally as a Social Worker, it got worse. As that was going on, alongside my fierce determination to succeed, there came also the thought, "at what?" and so began the doubts—about what I was doing, about the process, about myself personally—and yet I pressed onward for a long time.

This is normal, but the Great American Success Story is basically told as a fairly smooth ascent:

> *Meet Joe. Joe wants to be an astronaut. Joe studies math and science in school. He learns to fly a plane, and later joins the Air Force. He becomes the best pilot in his squadron, and applies to the astronaut program. He is accepted because of his amazing record. Joe flies into Earth orbit five times and goes to the Moon once. Joe gets medals of honor from the President and adulation everywhere.*

He has a lovely wife, 2.3 kids and half a dog. He lives in a three-bedroom ranch house outside of Houston, where everything is lovely and peaceful. Joe retires at age 59 and regales everyone in his family and social life about his great adventures.

You, too, can be like Joe.

But our own life pursuits do not match this steady ascent. Because we are never supposed to doubt ourselves and our purpose, we soldier on, but nothing improves for many of us. Then, the deep discouragement comes and the whole dream seems to break down. We end up feeling depressed, lost, confused, and angry at ourselves or others around us because the Great American Success Story for some blasted reason has not come true for us.

So, what do we do? Some of us go to Barnes and Noble or Amazon and look for books on how to succeed. There are so many of these. Some are great, and some are sheer tripe, but we do not know which ones work and which ones don't. After perhaps some advice, we try one, but we give up on the process before page ten. For many of us, what we have just read is like Joe's story all over again, told by people who are making a great deal of money off our misery, because they made their success while we do not succeed.

Does this sound familiar to you? It certainly was my story. It was like someone was lying to me the whole time, and I felt the results, while being afraid to believe that maybe something bigger and more systemic was wrong.

When I faced the facts, I found out that this is actually the case. And when I faced this, when I began to find out how to actually change the way I lived and how to have what I always sought but never exactly knew how to get, everything changed.

That is what this book is about. If that interests you and you want to find out what is going on and what to do, read on!

the big, fat
SUCCESS LIE

Don't worry. This is not going to be a rant against the evils of worldly success. But in order to fix the problem, we must begin to see the problem for what it truly is.

Now, any time someone wants to follow a path to success, there is an incentive for following that path. We are usually shown results in other people's lives that we want for ourselves, and we are attracted to the notion that we will be just like these success stories around us. We want to win.

The interesting thing is that this idea applies equally well to the pursuit of material, emotional, relational, and spiritual success. There's nothing wrong with having success in any (or many) of these areas. I have people in my life who are amazing success stories. I learn everything I can from them so that I might be able to do what they do, and I have had successes myself. This book draws on the wisdom of many, and those people constitute the "we" you'll hear mentioned throughout the book.

But our pursuit of success in the usual manner starts to fade when we realize a few things are going on:

- Our lifestyle must change in certain ways to allow success.

- We do not know everything.

- There are obstacles to our success, some of which are extraordinarily painful, such as family pressure, disdain from friends and colleagues, and, of course, our own egos.

Many of us have seen a motivational poster that says this: "Obstacles are the things we see when we take our eyes off the goal."

This saying is true enough, but it is not sufficient for us to just use this and succeed, or we would have already done it. Right? In actuality, there is a much bigger set of problems taking place with many of us, particularly Americans, because of what we believe life should be like. We believe there should be a particular—and straight—path from the beginning of our Great Work to the success.

Because we do not understand reality correctly, I, and many others like me, have at times fallen into a place I am going to call "the Messy Middle," when things aren't going as planned and negative emotions run high. We now need to talk about this, so that we can expose the lie and be set free of it.

the messy middle
EXPLAINED

The Messy Middle is an increasingly troubling aspect of one's drive for success in today's world. To some extent, this problem is actually quite new to us, and reflects many of the pressing problems in our time—spiritually, psychologically, and emotionally. All of this ends up creating a powerful physical manifestation that can cripple our work and efforts to succeed.

If we are to tackle this problem, it means that we must necessarily look at the factors that have made it the problem it is today. We will have to face these factors as they arise in ourselves, and change them. For some of us, this is going to be difficult work, because the needed change will challenge everything we think we know about ourselves and about life. But we can take heart.

The solution we seek does not lie in some new idea for the 21st century, but through a simple historical reflection and observation of times and people in the past. For the issue of Messy Middle situations, one of the most ancient sources—Holy Scripture—offers us many examples of people faced with adversity in accomplishing very difficult goals, and the texts also very clearly point out how those people were able to accomplish what they needed to do.

The solutions applied by these people are absolutely certain to work in our time and culture as well. In fact, we could say that no other solution really can be expected to work other than what is offered in the stories we find in the Bible. And far from just a verbal declaration of "Jesus!" we will be forced to face the reality of what it is to have and live by faith in the living God.

If you are ready for a stiff dose of reality and centering, read on!

In the 21st century, we have more access to information about other people and events in the space of a few minutes than our ancestors faced in several years, or even lifetimes. The Internet has united the world, but it has not pacified it. It has not lifted people's sense of one another to be like the "common brotherhood of man," by any means; nor has it made morality or respect for God any worse.

What it has done is to make all the information about what is going on in the world around us available immediately, with almost no safeguard to keep somebody from getting too much information, or information that is destructive to his or her soul and psyche. Before the Internet, of course, communication via television and radio existed, but the Internet put the crowning touch on "instant" information. Where we used to watch a single 30-minute broadcast to learn all the news we were going to take in for that day, now we have a continuous, almost real-time news cycle from almost everywhere in the world, at any time.

One of the effects of this is that we become accustomed to the idea that things happen very quickly in life. How often have we heard, "The world is moving so fast now, I can't keep up!" in our conversations?

This is largely illusory. While we have access to many things that are happening, things aren't actually happening any faster than they did before. However, it is easy to get the idea that many accomplishments that other people have happen swiftly and easily. We hear the story of the talented kid who has a platinum CD at the age of 15, or of the shooting-star startup that is responsible for the latest technological breakthrough, or how someone made a million dollars at nine years old. We read books that give success formulas and make it all seem so easy.

All of these stories may be true, but they are unusual, and they become news because they are unusual and sensational. Also, according to Malcolm Gladwell in his book *Outliers*, those stories are misleading because they leave out the Messy Middle (my term, not his). He makes it clear that they don't tell the whole story. Hearing about *so many* unusual items all at once creates a false belief that we, too, must be able to accomplish amazing things with great speed and no effort. And if we don't, there must be something wrong with us.

In such a climate of information, when we undertake our own effort and our own project—our own Great Work—it is easy to think that the results will come swiftly and without much effort. After all, the people we see in the news all the time are having this happen to them, right?

Wrong.

When our work seems to bog down, and things go slowly (if at all), this invites both frustration and discouragement, as we compare our progress with the success story of our choosing, and find our own to be lacking. Even incremental successes that we make are either overblown in our minds as we tell ourselves, "Now, things will *really* begin to happen!" or they are ignored because they are not huge and perfect. We might not pay attention to our progress at all, because what we have is not the final product we are seeking.

Here, now, are the symptoms of the Messy Middle, the Four Ds.

- **Distorted thinking–especially in terms of expected results not matching actual results**

- Dramatic emotional states–swings from euphoria to despair with not much in between

- Distraction by success stories around us and in the news, which also get us discouraged

- Dread of trying, of failing (and even of succeeding) at our endeavors

Where do we turn to deal with these emotional, spiritual, and psychological states? Often, to books like this one, or to other people, or to church, or to motivational seminars. And what do we hear in most of these?

Well, often, what we hear is more of the same kind of stuff we hear and see on the TV and Internet—stories of what amount to "instant" success. Further, if there was a struggle someone had, somehow it's never clear just how truly difficult that struggle was. This is because in less than an hour, contained in one episode, the struggle is resolved and everything is wonderful (at least according to the story being told). Life is not a show. It doesn't occur to us that some of these people struggled for *years*, and we are seeing only a very condensed snapshot of their lives in this time.

Shockingly, this is made even worse by some of the things we hear in our places of worship! Now, do not misunderstand here. This book stresses a Scripturally-based solution to this problem, but if we understand holy writings properly and usefully, we find that there are some modern teachings that do not stand up to what we find in ancient wisdom. Without getting into any more theology than needed, let us offer you this thought:

"Jesus Christ—the same yesterday,
today, and forever."

This thought was from the Apostle Paul in Hebrews (13:8), and it has a supporting context which is also vital to understanding both the Messy Middle and the solution to it:

Keep on loving each other as brothers and sisters. [a] 2 Don't forget to show hospitality to strangers, for some who have done this have entertained angels without realizing it! 3 Remember those in prison, as if you were there yourself. Remember also those being mistreated, as if you felt their pain in your own bodies. 4 Give honor to marriage, and remain faithful to one *another in marriage. God will surely judge people who are immoral and those who commit adultery. **5** Don't love money; be satisfied with what you have. For God has said, "I will never fail you. I will never abandon you." [b] **6** So we can say with confidence, "The Lord is my helper, so I will have no fear. What can mere people do to me?" [c] **7** Remember your leaders who taught you the word of God. Think of all the good that has come from their lives, and follow the example of their faith. **8** Jesus Christ is the same yesterday, today, and forever. **9** So do not be attracted by strange, new ideas. Your strength comes from God's grace, not from rules about food, which don't help those who follow them.*

Now here is the thought to consider as we go forward: If Christ is the same yesterday, today, and forever, then so is His word, and so is His Law. That last sentence, then, "Be not carried about with diverse and strange doctrines" tells us a great and simple truth. Diverse, strange, and "new" doctrines about how to live life are all over the place. But, if the Lord is the same at all times, then such ideas, which are always changing, are probably not correct and can do damage if we try to follow them.

The Messy Middle comes from our efforts to follow strange and diverse new doctrines, perhaps expressed sort of "below the surface" in ideas like these below:

- God wants you to succeed in the worldly sense (financially, socially, even sexually)

- God wants to do everything you want to do; He just wants you to take Him with you.

- If you are not wealthy and/or healthy, something is wrong with your relationship to God.

- If you are following God's will, even "struggle" is not difficult.

God made you *so good* that you cannot ever really make a mistake.

- If you do make a mistake, God is not with you because otherwise you would not have made the mistake. In other words, if you are struggling, you have already failed, and are, in fact, a failure.

Added to these are many ideas of what a "successful" life "looks like" and this image is always highly materialistic. Big car, big house, big money, and so on. In addition to material goods, it may involve prestigious positions at work and in society. For a married person, it may include having a spouse who looks like the most attractive movie star and does everything just right.

Even some church communities spread these ideas and present them as "gospel teaching." You can have your very own piece of the pie—for a price. Unfortunately, the only ones who seem to really profit from such a message are the people who give it. They are often very good motivational speakers, but they are far from telling the truth about living a life of real success. The price we pay in our donations to "the cause" creates wealthy motivational speakers and preachers, but little else.

We propose that all these ideas are, and have always been, completely incorrect. They have no basis in Scriptural wisdom that withstands honest evaluation. Even though there are passages in the Bible which talk about great blessings given to those who serve the Lord, there is no guarantee of worldly wealth and power for doing so. In fact, this is often quite the opposite of what actually happens. God is not against financial wealth, and He does empower us to prosper, but He is more concerned with the state of our hearts and souls than that of our bank accounts, and believing certain things can set us up for a Messy Middle and other problems.

We will look now at a figure from sacred history who had a challenge that was life-changing. He took it on and mastered it. We will look at what he did and then rather brutally contrast his way of living with our own.

REFLECTION:

Have you ever believed some of these below-the-surface ideas?

What was the outcome of believing them?

nehemiah's
STORY

Nehemiah was of the tribe of Judah, and he was raised in one of the periods of Israel's exile, in Syria. As a young man, he became a servant of the Persian court, eventually receiving the great honor of being the cupbearer for King Artaxerxes of Persia. This position was quite high, and it afforded Nehemiah direct and close access to the king. He earned this position because of his qualities of devotion, loyalty, honesty, and integrity.

Although Jerusalem had been destroyed, at the time of Nehemiah, about fifty thousand of the Jews had been allowed to return from their exile, and they were living in the ruined city. They had returned with the intent to rebuild the temple, but there had been much opposition to their work from all directions—internal strife, pressure from adversary tribes and people in the region, and fear of threat from the outside.

The walls were still in ruins, so the city was unprotected, and the reconstruction of the temple had only been completed with great difficulty, but even with the completion of the temple, the state in which the Jews lived was such that they were the laughingstock of the region. The city walls remained in shambles, and so the city and its inhabitants were under constant threat that even what they had been able to put together would be surely destroyed in a very small amount of time.

Of course, not only were the Jewish people objects of ridicule for the others in the region, but their God was also the object of ridicule. After all, what kind of god would be so weak and pathetic as to leave his followers in such conditions? This was the reasoning of the adversaries of Israel at the time. And because of this, it is important to realize that the Jews were not attacked simply because *they were not considered to be any threat or power in the area.* It was as if to say, "Sure, they have their ruined city and their temple, but they're like homeless people living on a pile of garbage."

There was no reason to even attack such people, because their humiliation was so bad already that they were losers, and their God, by extension, was also a loser.

Nehemiah received news of the state of the city from his relatives and he was saddened to the core about it, so much so that the King of Persia asked him what was on his heart, and so he told the king. He wanted to go to Jerusalem to fix the walls and make the city safe, so he asked the king for his blessing to do this, and also for help with the necessary materials to do the rebuilding.

Now, consider that Nehemiah was pretty serious about this idea—he had been fasting, praying, and mourning for his brothers and sisters in the afflicted city. So, this was not an idle charitable pursuit; this was something that changed Nehemiah's whole outlook on life. He was completely committed to this mission to rebuild Jerusalem's walls.

Once he got to Jerusalem, he saw with his own eyes the condition of the city and of the people living there. He also saw the adverse forces that both mocked and intimidated the citizens of Jerusalem. He faced all these adversities, and it was not an easy task by any means. Lots of work. Lots of struggle. However, Nehemiah's single-mindedness of purpose in his dedication to fulfilling the will of God allowed for his groups of people to organize and rebuild the walls in a very short time—only fifty-two days.

So, we have told the story about what happened, and it sounds like one of the typical Great American Success Stories, but what about the "Messy Middle" for Nehemiah? It seems from this retelling that *there was no such time*. But there *was* a struggle. Now we are going to look at this story as it relates to the context of our own lives as we struggle to do good things.

nehemiah's story
IN CONTEXT

A Template for Dealing with Obstacles

For those of us who wish to make a major change or to become successful, this level of conviction is also way beyond the moderate interest of a hobby; in fact, we often call this drive a "passion." The dream and desire become central to our lives and we put everything we have into this work.

Nehemiah had his conviction and he had the blessing of the king. He had prayed and was sure that this task was God-pleasing, and he even had this physically manifested by the fact that the king gave letters to him to other regional kings, who gave

Nehemiah all the materials he needed to rebuild Jerusalem's walls. And so he set off to Jerusalem and began the work.

Now, in our usual thoughts about people doing work for God's sake, which Nehemiah certainly was, we succumb all too easily to the idea that *because the work is God-pleasing, it will be an easy success.* And indeed, regarding Nehemiah's story, this does seem to be the case—at first. After all, a *pagan* king heard Nehemiah's plea, and blessed him, and supplied him with what he needed. Certainly this was a miracle of God because pagan people did not usually have a high opinion of these strange people who insisted on devoting themselves to only one God. Further, the people of Israel were still mostly in exile and were a ridiculed nation, so again, the manifestation of God's grace is profoundly evident at this point in the story. So, Nehemiah had an easy time of it, right?

Wrong.

When Nehemiah began to rebuild the wall, he did inspire some people to help him do so. The project seemed to go well until about halfway through it. But word spread everywhere about what these people were undertaking, and so, naturally, the enemies of Israel were quick to speak up about it and about their opposition to the rebuilding of Jerusalem's walls. These people—Sanaballat, Tobia, and Gesam—not only opposed Nehemiah's work, they also verbally attacked him. They said he was doing it all out of self-interest and they accused him of being disloyal to the ruling king of that land. That was probably a frightening accusation, even though Nehemiah was operating with the express blessing of the king.

So began Nehemiah's struggle. There was real opposition to his Great Work. We can relate this struggle to our own Messy Middle. The opposition from the outside was not fun, but it was understandable and expected. After all, a walled Jerusalem would withstand attack and be a very strong city, and this was a threat to the adversarial groups of people that until then had discounted Israel as a "has-been" group of people, not even worthy of worry.

But the strife did not stop there. The wall was *really* destroyed. The stones were scorched, and there were piles of broken stone and rubbish everywhere. The conditions were so bad that to even look at that mess must have been discouraging to the people there, for they had not been able to tackle the job of rebuilding it. Even those working on the wall got worried because it was in such bad shape.

Pressure was mounting from all sides, and the pressure increased day by day. The attacks of the enemy became heavier and more intense the more progress Nehemiah made. Nehemiah and the inhabitants of Jerusalem prayed to God for safety, and they set up security to protect their work.

Now, many of us are presented with major crises in our lives, and some are very sudden and frightening. A tornado comes, or there arises a sickness that is severe, or a market crash in our segment of industry occurs. These are indeed sudden and unexpected, and they require great perseverance and faith to get through. But what about this sort of "creeping crisis," which starts not because of a bad event, but because of the attempt to accomplish a good one?

In case after case, when someone has a driving mission to accomplish in life, even some of their closest relatives and friends will oppose what they are doing. Mohandas K. Gandhi's wife is depicted as opposing her own husband's efforts to create a community of brotherhood. Job was encouraged by his own wife to give up, curse God, and die, rather than do what Job was doing, which was to pray and continually trust God even though everything good in his life had been stripped away for a long time. Israel wandered in the wilderness for forty years, and Moses, their leader, had only the promise of the Lord that they would pass to a better land—but even he himself would not enter it.

With any worthwhile attempt, there is inevitably some period of extended daily struggle, where things may be moving forward, but there is little to zero joy, little sign of real accomplishment, and what seems like many steps backward. Recently Elon Musk's company, SpaceX, has been trying to land a first stage of their rocket upright on a barge in water. After a successful attempt to land on solid ground, the next number of test landings on a floating barge all failed. Many explosions and loss of a great amount of money were the result. It must have seemed at times that it was a hopeless pursuit. Why do upright landings?

Why do them on water? We can be sure that not a few people in SpaceX questioned the vision.

And so it was with Nehemiah. Not only was he in the middle, so were all the people who were working with him.

So, here, let us briefly examine some factors that were happening with Nehemiah.

He was experiencing multiple obstacles to doing the will of God:

- A discouraged workforce
- Mocking, threats, and offers of bribery from enemies
- The very difficult nature of the work itself–the city and her walls were absolutely in shambles
- A limitation on time (No project can be expected to be completed without some time limit.)
- Resistance due to his own fears

Four of these elements—a discouraged workforce, bribery, difficult work, and time—are all *external* difficulties that hindered Nehemiah's work.

As with any worthwhile endeavor, most projects have their share of difficulties in getting done. This has always been so throughout history. There are many recent examples. They include the building of the new airtight caissons used to build the towers of the Brooklyn Bridge in New York; the sequence of programs that helped the USA put a man on the moon, running from 1961 to 1969; the construction and marketing of the personal computer by Apple and then by IBM, and too many others to list. Anyone who reads the history of these ventures will find out how challenging all these were to the people working on them.

Most success manuals will do a fine job of helping aspiring entrepreneurs with how to face and negotiate these sorts of external difficulties. For the sake of focus, we are not going to address these matters much in this work. Here, we want to have a look at the remaining element of resistance that, in our view, kills most great projects and works before they ever really get off the ground. Just know that resistance should be expected.

Resistance is not necessarily something we want, and in fact, some of us go to great distances to avoid it, but it can be very good for us. Without resistance, we would never develop and grow. God gets the glory at the end—if we choose to keep going. Why should we give the enemy the satisfaction of winning, letting all of our efforts be in vain?

Of these above-listed elements of resistance, one appears to be an *internal* obstacle. And which one do you think might be the most critical? Yep, you got it. That internal one: "Resistance due to his own fears."

Now, there are other manifestations of this internal resistance, and some people may insist that all this is based on fear—fear of failure, or even fear of success, and multiple variations on these two themes. Now, this is indeed a factor, but there is something very important about Nehemiah and how he handled them.

He handled the most critical fear by not taking too much heed to what he thought or how he felt, but instead relying on faith about the purpose that he had—to rebuild the wall. In other words, rather than ponder the discouragement and the disappointments, *he never took his eye off God and the task which he believed God had given him to perform.*

REFLECTION:

What has been your greatest fear to overcome regarding achieving success?

What can you put in place today to push through?

Has resistance ever won in your life? What did you learn from it?

What will you do differently moving forward?

---

a look at
PURPOSE

We all have a purpose. What does it look like? People have a burning desire to figure out why they're here and what they're supposed to do. If you've ever asked, "Who am I and why am I here?" or "What should I do with my life?" then you are familiar with that need to find purpose. You know that you won't find fulfillment until you do.

The journey to discovering your purpose can be long and tiresome. Some daily habits will help you to be purposeful, starting today. Many people find it helpful to read these aloud every morning. You may find it helpful to put them on attractive sticky notes around your mirror or to set up a reminder in your phone.

Love on purpose. I will love not only those closest to me, but strangers as well. Even more challenging (yet greatly rewarding), I will love those who are against me. I will purpose today to especially love those who hurt me, oppose me, and spitefully use and abuse me (Luke 6:28, Matthew 5:44, 46–48).

Move on purpose. I will keep going, even when I feel like quitting. I will move with a purpose. I will work hard today. I will determine to seek solutions to challenges at work and with family. I will keep moving forward. I will move on when needed, or maybe change course or direction, but I will keep moving. I will not stop (Exodus 14:15–16 NLT).

Rest on purpose. I will allow myself to rest. This may seem contradictory to moving on purpose, but it's not. Resting is different than stopping. I will rest to sharpen my axe. I will enjoy my life and loved ones today. I will rest in the arms of a loved one, take a walk, meditate, and pray. I will rest in the divine love and guidance living within. I will appreciate that the ability to move with wisdom and love the unlovable only comes from rest and stillness. It is vital to rest on purpose (Psalm 37:7; Psalm 46:10; Hebrews 4:2–4).

Laugh on purpose. Laughter is great for the abs and the mood. Laughter is medicine to the whole person—mind, body, and spirit. I will not take myself or life too seriously (Psalm 126:2, Jeremiah 30:19).

Live on purpose. I will share my joy with others and remind myself of my blessings and thank God for what He has given me. I will remind myself to be thankful in all things and to be faithful with what I have been given. I will remember that my desire for more will only be satisfied when I am content with what I have—grateful for the blessings God has already given me. God will only give additional things when I am faithful in the little things. Only then will I be entrusted with more (1 Thessalonians 5:18, Psalm 23:5, Psalm 28:7, 1 Samuel 2:8, Zachariah 4:10, Phillipians 4:12, and Luke 16:10). To download a printout of these, go to http://www.movedbypurpose.net/resources/affirmations/

When our purpose is revealed to us, the enemy becomes threatened. He does not want us to reach our destiny and will do everything he can to distract and discourage everyone. Keeping our eyes on Christ and staying committed to and focused on our mission is vital. Saying what Nehemiah said when people tried to distract him is helpful: "I am doing a great work and I cannot come down. Why should the work stop while I leave it and come down to you?" (Nehemiah 6:3). He knew that their plan was to delay or stop the work he was doing. Staying committed as Nehemiah did goes a long way toward succeeding.

At first, I had no idea what I was getting into with fulfilling my purpose and building my business to accomplish it. And I thank God I didn't. I thought that because God had shown me what I was made for, it was going to be an effortless journey and everything would naturally come. Nothing could be further from the truth.

Had I seen everything that was ahead of me, I would never have stepped out in faith on the journey. The story of Nehemiah rebuilding the wall for Jerusalem is an excellent story that will encourage you through your transition from beginning to end of your Great Work.

Examining Our Purpose

Sometimes we think we've found our purpose, but we may be mistaken about something in relation to it. We may be in error when it comes to our thinking, beliefs, and attitudes. Being wrong regarding these things can easily cause the difficulties we have in achieving success. These errors have been taught to us in one way or another, and they must be exposed so we can really discern our actions more accurately. It's important to examine our purpose and to be certain that we are on the right path.

Pondering a couple of interesting and critical matters will be helpful.

1. *What is the will of God?*

2. *How do I know this is so?*

Now, this is a brutal test. And, unfortunately for the sake of some of our passions, what comes next may seem like a letdown—indeed, almost a betrayal—of what we have been told is the American Dream about career and living a great life and so on. However, we are introducing this idea not to discourage but to help make sense out of this problem and to find excellent solutions.

There are some questions we should ask ourselves, to check our honesty about an idea we have:

1. Is the goal bigger than we ourselves are?

Many times the goal we set for ourselves is directly tied to our own comforts. We wish for a good income and an easy life, and we think that our pet idea is the sure way to get there. But does our idea have any impact beyond this? Are we simply looking for ways out of hard or unpleasant work, or ways to line our pockets, or are we actually seeing something bigger, something better and more significant than we ourselves are, which we want to go after?

Nehemiah was grieved not for his own welfare; after all, his own personal welfare was fine. As the king's cupbearer, he held a high, honorable, trusted and high-paying position in his life. There was no need, on the basis of personal security, to undertake anything like that rebuilding project.

But Nehemiah was thinking far beyond himself. He was thinking of his displaced people, the nation of Israel; he was thinking of the God who had chosen this wayward people; and he was thinking of the humiliation of his countrymen and God. Remember, in those days, there was a rather direct assumption that the mightiest god was the one that won everything, so the God of Israel was understood as weak by the outsider powers around Israel, because there was no longer a temple, nor a Holy City, for a long time. Even once the temple was rebuilt, the rest of the city was in such a bad physical state that any invading army could have destroyed the temple easily.

So, Nehemiah wanted to correct this problem. He knew that his God was not some pitiable weakling. He cared about the honor of his people and he cared even more about the repentance and rebirth of his nation. It was a big undertaking. And it is worth noting that he asked a pagan king for the blessing to go rebuild his own nation, *and he got that blessing.*

Being resurgent does not have to mean resurgent as a conquering power; it can mean *restoring respect*.

2. Is the goal God-pleasing?

Again, this is a tough question in our times, because we do not think about what is God-pleasing in the way Nehemiah did. Nehemiah thought about this in terms of knowing his nation's history, the fact that they have been chosen as the people to bear witness to the One God, Creator of all that is, and that in returning to their senses after following pagan gods, the people of Israel and Judah were still the chosen people and were still called to bear witness to God's existence.

But in 21st Century America, quite frankly, we do not usually think about this matter at all. We have gradually gotten the matter of "God-pleasing" to really mean "me-pleasing." We have gotten to this place through accepting a series of teachings that sound nice but are utterly false and nonsensical.

One very popular notion in our times is the message that "God wants you to be rich and healthy, and to have the abundant life." This is often said, nearly word-for-word as written here. Of course the corollary of this is that a lack of wealth, health, or abundance must, by definition, mean that one is *not* living by God's will. That might not be true for each person in that situation. It doesn't take into consideration the fact that there are sometimes difficult seasons in our lives that are meant to teach us (or those who see us) crucial lessons—and that is God's will.

The wrong kind of thinking creates a really nasty setup for many of us, because many of us are certainly not wealthy. Some of us have health issues. Some of us find life difficult. It is made worse by our incredible propensity to compare our lives to those of people around us, who have (seemingly) attained a greater degree of success than we have. When this comparison takes place, we usually lose. If we are very prideful, we pick people *we* think are "losers" and elevate ourselves above them. The fact remains that when we look at our accomplishments in comparison to even these supposed "lowlifes," we might have more things, but we still lose in other ways. Maybe these "losers" are happier than we are (probably because they do not compare their lives to others' lives) and maybe the "winners" are living in a house of cards, beautiful as it may be, yet doomed to collapse, while we are ignoring the blessings we have in our own lives.

Take for example, Don, a high-level executive making a handsome six-figure income. From the world's perspective, he had everything—a good job, nice house, power, status, etc. When working with Don, he admitted that one summer he was looking out his kitchen window at the guys mowing the lawn. He said, "I'd give anything to trade places with them." He felt that they were free—they were able to enjoy the beauty of nature every day, run their own company, and have control over their time. At least that's what he thought. I wonder if those guys cutting his lawn felt the same way about him. Perhaps they thought, *wouldn't it be nice to live in this big, beautiful house and neighborhood and work from home?*

Samantha is another example of someone who put her time in, paid her dues, and worked her way all the way to the top of an organization—to only get so burned out she couldn't bear one more day. When I spoke to Samantha, she cried, "I just want to stock shelves somewhere. I want to do something where

I don't have to make all the decisions and think so hard. I need to allow my mind to rest and check out. I made it all the way to the top and I don't want it."

But here's the kicker—Nehemiah did not give any thought to his prosperity or lack thereof, nor did he compare himself or his work to anyone else.

When we consider this, this shows that we have added something to what we think the gospel message is, but it is nothing but a pure burden to our success.

Nehemiah was of one focus. He knew that the walls of the Holy City must be rebuilt to keep the city and temple safe. Nothing else mattered. His personal prosperity, or judging himself by the outcome around him, or by his popularity, or how he felt—none of these mattered. For Nehemiah, the *only* outcome that mattered was that the walls of Jerusalem got rebuilt.

For us, the tendency to go elsewhere and to think about other people and our "progress" and personal welfare as compared to theirs creates an enormous internal set of obstacles. Even if what we are doing was God-pleasing at the outset, we become lost in our own self-centered mess of thinking. Comparing ourselves to others and holding our progress up to their progress only leads to problems. And social media doesn't help. In fact, recent studies have found that heavy social-media use can cause depression:

- Exposure to highly idealized representations of peers on social media elicits feelings of envy and the distorted belief that others lead happier, more successful lives than we do.

- Engaging in activities of little meaning on social media may give a feeling of "time wasted" that negatively influences mood.

- Social-media use could be fueling "Internet addiction," a proposed psychiatric condition closely associated with depression.

- Spending more time on social media may increase the risk of exposure to cyber-bullying or other similar negative interactions, which can cause feelings of depression.

That mess is not God-pleasing.

But sometimes we also find ourselves thinking a lot about a project after we get into it, and there is a different set of thoughts that we go through. Rather than comparing ourselves to others, sometimes there is the nagging sense that our wish is something that is radically self-serving. And yet, we're told by some famous figures that this is precisely what we should be doing. After all, they tell us, "God wants this for you."

Now, we can be sure of God's love for us, and that his intent for all His creation—especially for the human segment of that creation—is to live lives that are greatly blessed. But wait a second. Are "blessed" and "happy" the same?

And the answer is . . . No, they are not. But, why, then, do we see things like "Happy are those who are persecuted" in our Bibles? (Matt. 5:10, TLB, GNT). Or in Psalms, some of us may encounter, "Happy is the man who does not walk in the advice of the wicked" (Psalm 1:1, CSB).

The problem is unfortunate, but it is very simple. "Happy" there is a misinterpretation. We can give the benefit of the doubt and say it was by accident, but the result is the same: the meaning isn't exact. "Blessed" would be more accurate.

Now, while it is true that many times while we are being blessed, we are happy, this is not always so. John the Baptist was probably not very happy being in the prison cell and probably did not think getting beheaded was going to be a great time. He may well have rejoiced, knowing he had fulfilled his work that God had given him, but this is a very unpleasant scene.

Jesus Himself, too, beat to a bloody pulp by the lash of the Romans, being put in a horrible prison cell, falsely accused, and then crucified by His own creations. Happy? Probably not.

Even in modern times—Dr. Martin Luther King. Was he doing God's will? Absolutely. Did he enjoy the bullet he received for it? Probably not.

We need to understand that the modern notion of "happiness" is also a big trap for many of us. We are told that if we are doing what God's will is for us, then we will be happy. And there *are* times this is true. But there are also times when it's awful. When we are trudging through and everything in life seems as worthless as sand, we are still called to continue in our work because it's more important than how we feel or think. Struggles will come. It's part of the territory when accomplishing a Great Work. Perseverance is needed.

This state of pushing onward with the conviction that what we are doing is something of God is a blessed state. There is enormous strength to be drawn on in such situations because they really *are* of God quite often.

What if you are sure it is the right thing, but you lack the resources to bring it about? Trusting in God's provision to get you through is tough sometimes, but be encouraged. God is the one who created you to accomplish and fulfill a specific purpose. He already gave you permission to build something. Not only that, but if you are on course, He will also provide the resources, even if it feels like you don't have everything you think you need. He will provide.

3. Is our goal self-referenced?

Sometimes we are dealing with much more self-referenced goals, and one of the signs that God gives us that this is the case is the nagging feeling that something is wrong, or He grants us failure after failure. While such things can happen even if we are on the right track, we have to examine our motives for what we are doing. The chance is that if the main beneficiaries to our great plans are just ourselves, we may well be off the mark.

The problem with some of the messages of *self-affirmation* is precisely that these teachings do not really point us to God; they point us inward to our own egos and toward our own temporal desires.

It is incorrect thinking to believe that God wants us to have success on earth so we can enjoy life (and for *no further purpose*.) The mark of those who truly faced and did God's will is that their work often did not really make their lives more comfortable, although sometimes it did; usually their work improved the lives of those around them. We have some Biblical references, such as the account of Lydia, the seller of purple, who is mentioned in the book of Acts.

Lydia was a wealthy merchant woman. She used her wealth, in part, to support a congregation of Christian believers in her area, even donating the use of her house to serve as a meeting place, a church, for those people. That is hard work, and even more so then, when an average Church service would last for five hours or longer. There were probably times that were very tough for Lydia, and where things might have been difficult and even unpleasant. But she is not remembered for the difficulty she faced. She is remembered for offering her home as a church. In other words, like Nehemiah, she understood that the calling itself is the blessing, and to fulfill it is also a blessing. She was probably happy at times, but that is beside the point, which is *the mission was what mattered*.

So, when we get a nagging sense that something might be wrong with our "dream pursuit," it is a good idea to look into this. While ideally it is best to determine at the beginning whether our grand idea is God-pleasing, it is also something we can usually stop and re-evaluate at any time.

How Do We Determine Whether We Are On the Right Track?

How do we really determine if an idea is God-pleasing, and if it is also God-pleasing for us to take it on personally? After all, it's easy to be deceived, and discerning the voice of God can be difficult. Seeking counsel from others who have more experience with following God's will is the best course. It involves approaching them with complete honesty and humility, laying everything out on the table and holding nothing back. We let them have a look at our idea. Then we listen.

By doing this, we seek to avoid the trap of delusion. We may be deluded by ideas from our culture. We may delude ourselves out of selfish ambition. We may also be deluded by the enemy, who twists God's word and can masquerade as the voice of God. He knows Scripture better than people do.

We like to pound down any nagging feeling that we're on the wrong track, because we do not usually want to be humble enough to admit we are wrong and that we need to change course. This is also a good reason to seek counsel *before* engaging in a new pursuit, because once we've invested our heart, soul, and time into it, it is hard to give up, even when everything inside and outside of us is screaming that it's wrong.

But if we do have counsel, and that counsel has shown us that our intent is right, then we can place a lot of faith in the idea that this idea is God-pleasing because it was verified by someone who does pretty well at serving God, and who knows us pretty well, too. Sometimes a person God has put in our lives will say exactly what we need to hear, exactly when we need to hear it. It's our job to listen for it, then listen to it.

Then, we begin to match the place that Nehemiah was actually in when he asked his king for counsel. Here we can be impressed by the fact that although the king was not an Israelite (and, further, was pagan), the king also knew Nehemiah, loved him, and understood that if Nehemiah thought it was important to serve this God, then it must be important.

Not everyone who gives good counsel has to be a Christian believer to be able to give good advice to those of us who are Christians. God sometimes throws a twist into the deal and gives us help from amazing and unexpected sources. And we can see that this probably helped Nehemiah even more, for his faith in God was *verified* by the response his pagan boss gave him: "Go, and let me help you!"

REFLECTION:

Have you ever convinced yourself that an idea was God-inspired when it really wasn't?

Have you ever gotten some great counsel from an unexpected source?

emotional and
mental obstacles
RE-EXAMINED

In Light of Our Our Discussion

We've looked at Nehemiah's story and compared and contrasted his experiences with those we may be having. What may seem a point of interest is that we have talked about doubt and faith, and how to work with them to discern God's will for us, especially in regard to our personal plans and ideas.

What we have not really talked about are emotional states—we have touched on them, but not focused much on them.

Why is this? After all, the Messy Middle is primarily an emotional state. It does not really deal with how our project is proceeding so much as it does with *how we feel about it and about ourselves.*

This is an extremely central point that we must consider if we are to have the victory we want.

Nehemiah's story covers several pages in the Bible. The wall took fifty-two days to rebuild. Now, that is very short, and indeed, it is a miraculous effort. But, fifty-two days is still fifty-two days. It takes fifty-two days to get through them. What Scripture does not record is all the potential for internal doubt and struggle that Nehemiah could have faced.

The story of Nehemiah records two points where Nehemiah faced an emotional state that was difficult. Both times were in the beginning of the story. One was when Nehemiah found out the state of the people living in Jerusalem, and the welfare of the city itself. This story was so grievous that it brought Nehemiah to tears, and he wept, mourned, and fasted and prayed to God, asking the Lord for forgiveness for his people's sins.

The second time was after he prayed to God to be attentive to the cry of his servants, the repentant people of Israel, and he had occasion to appear before his own master, the King Artaxerxes. The king saw that Nehemiah was sad and troubled and asked him about it, because he had never seen his servant in such a state before. And Nehemiah said, "Then I was very sore afraid" and when the king asked what he wanted, Nehemiah goes on to say, "So, I prayed to the God of heaven. And I said unto the king . . ." and he told the king his request.

Let's pay some attention to this. The rebuilding of the wall and all the issues that concerned it, the time taken, and the opposition from adversaries are met by no emotional highlight from Nehemiah. It is very possible he felt afraid or threatened, or other things, but he never mentions them. Yet, where he does mention an emotional state, his response is very consistent.

He prays, and he faces reality. It is interesting to note that the only place where Nehemiah mentions fear is when the opportunity to actually begin is placed before him, that is, when the king asked him what was bothering him.

Now, our Messy Middle contains a plethora of mental and emotional states—and often it may seem that the emotional and mental tangle is so huge that the only solution seems to be to withdraw from the idea and stop trying. This is a big mess, but if we contrast it to Nehemiah's story, we do not see this mess there. We *do* see a lot of opposition from adverse powers, but we do not find a problem with Nehemiah's emotional state. At every turn, he faces each challenge with wisdom, honesty, and prayer.

When it happens to us, we need to recognize it for what it is and fight it. We pull out our sword (God's Word) and speak against it. We put up our shield of faith to deflect the fiery arrows of doubt. We are all in a battle, and we must fight. The victory is already ours; we just have to defend that victory. Jesus has already overcome the trials and tribulations we will face; however, that doesn't mean we sit back and take whatever comes our way.

The story of Nehemiah states that the builders slept in their working clothes and had their sword in one hand, hammer in the other. They were focused and working on the task at hand, at the same time fully aware and prepared for an attack of the enemy. We who have succeeded had this kind of focus, determination, and gumption to see our purpose through. Negative thoughts like the following may occur to anyone:

- You are wasting your time doing this.

- No one will care and your efforts do not matter. In fact, you don't matter.

- Your work will never have any meaning or value.

- What a joke to think you actually will meet your goals.

- You will fail. Just give up. Come down and stop what you are doing.

Those thoughts must be countered with truth and action. Those of us who have courage are not saying we have no fear. We just push through it. We do it afraid.

This is what it takes! We must rise up and set ourselves up for success. What action are you taking today to meet your destiny, calling, and purpose?

Earlier, we highlighted several factors that lead to what we call the Messy Middle, which is the problem of bad thinking and emotions during the time of struggle on the way to success. Those factors are essentially centered in our own ego, whether that ego be something we are trying to stroke through our specific desire and vision of what "success" should be for us, or the self-centered fear that comes from having no verifiable faith in our direction.

We have also identified the antidote to this— checking our idea to see whether it is God-pleasing, whether it serves others or only ourselves, whether the goal is bigger than ourselves, and whether it is even the right effort for us at this time; and seeking counsel from someone experienced in this way of life to check our thinking.

These simple questions and counsel are enormously powerful ways to help us get out of the psychological and emotional mess that are characteristic of the 21st century version of the Messy Middle. Now we will look a little more at how true this is.

Fear

"Is this going to work?"

"How can I do this?"

"Is this right or wrong?"

"Should I be doing this?"

The questions can go on, ad nauseam. Look familiar? All of these are manifestations of fear and its associated thinking. No doubt you, as the reader, will come up with your own variations on this theme. More than any other thing, fear can hold us back from living victoriously in this life (if we let it).

The modern analysis of fear uses the very word as an acronym, with meanings like "False Evidence Appearing Real," "Forget Everything And Run," or "Face Everything And Rise" and other anecdotal sayings that are all valid in their own contexts. But the power to actually deal with this does not come from saying a bunch of magic words. That is like trying to lift ourselves off the ground by pulling up on our own bootstraps, and even though we've been told our entire lives that pulling ourselves up by our own bootstraps is the way to become a success, that is an absurd impossibility.

The power to beat this fear comes only from faith. A saying that can be helpful when fear tries to rise up and stop us is "Fear and faith cannot occupy the same space." Now, that faith is a challenge, because we say we believe in God, but we may sense that "faith" is a different animal because we cannot seem to make ourselves *feel* faithful.

That is because faith is not a feeling. Faith is belief put into practice. If we are using only ourselves and our desire as the source material for our belief, we are probably not going to get very far. After all, where is our Messy Middle coming from? Ourselves. So trying to fix ourselves by ourselves is silly; even more bluntly, it is insane.

But faith in God, or in the counsel of someone who has experience in following God's will, is enormously helpful to us. When I have doubted my efforts at my own work, I have found that talking to my mentor will undo hours of worry with only one or two sentences from him. He will say very directly what the truth is and what I ought to be doing (or not doing), and then all I have to do is trust that counsel and follow it. Then, fear is relegated to an occasional feeling, but it has no power to paralyze, because I am simply following instructions.

In Nehemiah's case, isn't that what he did? He prayed to God for forgiveness for his people, and then asked for the opportunity to do something about the problem they faced. Then God granted that through the question of the king, "What is wrong?" and Nehemiah simply faced the fact that there was his doorway opened to him, and he took a leap of faith that this was God's answer to his prayers, as in fact it turned out to be. The king's response showed God's grace in action at the temporal level, and Nehemiah was able to put even stronger faith in the knowledge he was on the right track, because God moved the heart of his pagan boss to act on behalf of the people of Israel—which is a miracle.

When we seek counsel and when we have verified our purpose is God-pleasing, this creates a lot of support for us. Everything else is just logistics, one foot in front of the other.

Now, this does not mean that we only seek counsel one time for our project. The Messy Middle problem tends to recur in us when we've had a lot of time by ourselves to think about things. This is when our ego steps in with its characteristic self-inflation or self-doubt and compares our progress (or even our projects) to some unreal ideal.

Doubt is the killer of faith. So, we have found it useful to check ourselves regularly with our mentors to make sure we are following instructions well, and that we are not making up new things that no one told us about, or believing the lies of the enemy.

Wise counsel is a very important factor, and it flies in the face of everything that 21st century American culture tells us. That culture says, "No one can tell me what to do" and indeed, try telling some other adult what they ought to do when they do not want advice, and you will see that it's true.

But the problem is precisely this—that when we only listen to ourselves, God is shut out. God often speaks through others. Even when God speaks directly to us, sometimes we do not listen well. But the advice of another person in confidence and counsel is good, and we may find ourselves facing things we do not like to hear but that we can absolutely trust.

REFLECTION:

When have you tried helping yourself by yourself? How did that work out for you?

Are your eyes open to God's answers? God's answers often require our action—and that action step may stretch you. Is there any action step you need to take to receive God's answer?

Despair and Discouragement

This test of our goal and counsel works on other emotional states, too, such as discouragement when things seem to be bogged down. Far from just hearing an encouraging word from friends who do not know the real nature of what we're doing, hearing the honest counsel of someone we have opened up to can simultaneously challenge us to excel and to resolve our discouraged feelings in just moments. Sometimes it takes longer, but that is usually because we are refusing to listen to the advice we are getting. Their encouragement to express gratitude will be especially important when things aren't going the way we want them to go.

It's hard to express gratitude when we don't get our way, but it's good for us to do it anyway. When nothing seems to be going right, it is difficult to praise God. Our attention is turned toward what we want and don't have, rather than focusing on all that we do have. It is not necessary (or helpful) to beat ourselves up when our strength seems insufficient and we begin to put our eyes on the resistance instead of on the Great Work we're doing to advance the Kingdom in some way. What is necessary is to just get the focus back where it needs to be.

It's easy to fall into condemnation if we have slipped, but it's important not to. We are all human, and perfect performance is not something God asks of us. He asks us for a perfect heart toward him. Just reading of the human imperfections of the heroes of the Bible (such as Solomon, David, Abraham, and Jacob) should be enough to convince us that God has done, still does, and will continue to do great things through imperfect people.

This knowledge alone should help prepare our hearts and minds to apply these five tips that will help us to get over not getting our own way.

First: Pray it out. For whatever reason, people often pray *after* they have tried a bunch of things. We recommend praying *first* and tapping into the wisdom of God to guide you to your solution. A solution and peace will come so much faster when this discipline is developed.

Second: Offer up a sacrifice of thanksgiving and praise. The last thing anyone wants to do is praise while facing disappointments, frustration, and stress. It's easy to get angry and bitter and to fall into self-pity when we have to face problems we don't want to deal with. This is why the Bible words it as "a sacrifice of praise." We have to sacrifice our own feelings and look at the positive.

Writing down a list of blessings in the midst of disappointment and frustrations can help with refocusing. Bringing to mind all that we have can begin to alleviate the negative emotions we are experiencing. So can taking a walk, working out, listening to positive/inspirational content, or taking a nap.

Third: Call on trusted friends and mentors. Sometimes we still feel icky after we have prayed and done our best to give thanks and praise. Calling and reaching out to a loved one who is good at supporting, listening, and comforting us is important at that time. Just knowing we are not alone and that we have people who love us and are supporting us can be enough to pull us out of the pit of despair. These people can remind us of the good in our lives and be able to offer sound solutions.

Fourth: Watch your words. When emotional and distraught about a situation, we can speak a whole lot of the wrong things. Take the time to speak differently. Are you financially struggling right now? Ask yourself how often you are saying these things: "I'm broke, I don't have any money, I can't afford to do anything I want," et cetera.

By repeatedly stating something, we repeatedly get that. If you are doing your part to change your financial situation so you have savings and you can afford to do the things you want to, but you are still having problems, you might want to check what comes out of your mouth. Speaking the scriptures over a situation and continuing to be faithful in our efforts to change our behavior brings about the harvest—in due season.

Fifth: Take action. Start taking action to solve the problem, one baby step at a time. The calmer we are, the more ground we can cover. If we start taking action in the height of our emotions, any more problems and obstacles may only stress us out further.

Waiting for a breakthrough for quite some time can make it difficult to want to praise God and thank Him for all that He is doing in your life. After all, you want what you want when you want it.

Why does God instruct us to give thanks always in His word? Scripture says to trust in the Lord with all your heart. Acknowledge Him in all your ways and He will make your paths straight.

God tells us to acknowledge Him, thank Him and praise Him, but it's not *for Him*. It benefits us. God is complete. He doesn't need our praise to feel good about Himself. Praise, thanksgiving, and acknowledgement of what God has done and is doing in our lives are for our own benefit. When you are not getting your way, you have a choice to make. Are you going to choose to fixate (aka meditate) on what you don't have yet? Or will you choose to take your eyes off of what you don't have yet and focus on what you already have?

In order to really help you nail this practice of thanksgiving and praise, ask yourself these questions every day:

What has God recently done for me that has really blessed me? Did you receive unexpected income? Have you recently benefited from a value-packed conversation with someone who generously gave their expertise and time away? Write down what God has blessed you with.

How has my life been changed since growing closer to God? As we grow closer in relationship with God, our old sinful nature dies off. We may have been a nasty person once, but not anymore. Maybe you used to scream at your kids over the pettiest things and now have much more control over your temper. Write down how God has transformed your life—and thank Him for it.

How has God shown up for you when there was no other way out? We have all experienced times where God has shown up big. Maybe you were pressed on all sides and there was no way out, but God—right on time and in His glory—made a way for you. Write that down, and give thanks for it.

Write down all the things you are grateful for today. Do you have shelter? Food? Good health? Children? A spouse? Good friends? A great church? An education? Warm water? Write down everything that you have that you typically take for granted. Thank God for His provision for your daily needs.

The point of these questions is to really open your eyes and change your perspective. When we zero in on the one thing we've been begging God relentlessly for and He still hasn't delivered on—that will put us in a sour, bitter attitude. Sure, share your heart with

Him. Express your disappointment. Cry out to Him for encouragement. But make sure you are praising Him and thanking Him for all He has done and all He will do for you. If nothing else, thank Him that because of Jesus' sacrifice you have a full inheritance in the Kingdom of God. Now that alone is enough to worship Him.

Helping someone else get what they want may be the perfect antidote to selfishness, which can rise up in us when we've been brooding. When we are going through a season of trial or barrenness, it is likely that there is little energy left over for anyone else. The cup is empty.

Sure, there are plenty of people in need, but you don't want to be bothered with them. You have your own needs to meet. After all, you need to take care of yourself first in order to be useful to anyone else, anyway. Right?

Here's what is wrong with the above thought process. I'm going to confess that this was my former thought process before I conquered it. There's a word for it. It's called selfishness.

Yes, it's easier to give from an overflowing cup. Yes, it is healthy to take care of oneself by saying no to others sometimes, by setting healthy boundaries, and by taking care of one's own needs first. Yes, the Bible says to "love your neighbor as yourself," not "love your neighbor more than you love yourself." That also means not to love yourself more than you love your neighbor. It's equal.

One of the best antidotes to discouragement and disappointment is serving someone. We spend time with someone who feels lonely. We visit homebound people and have meals with them. Being of service to someone is never regrettable.

Nehemiah had to live in sweet balance with both giving and receiving. He could not build that wall alone. He worked with a team of people. He also didn't give in to every request of every person. He had to set boundaries. Because of that, the wall of Jerusalem was rebuilt in a miraculous 52 days!

Being Overwhelmed

Being overwhelmed is something we all encounter. It can be difficult when that feeling hits us like a tidal wave. Our culture is so programmed to have every day be crammed full of activity. Once we become clear on our Great Work, it is critical to be focused all the way through the Messy Middle to the other side. Feeling overwhelmed regarding how big the work is can come at us quite often. So how do we deal with everything that needs to be completed?

We break down the big project into small, manageable steps. This is easier said than done. Seeing a clear vision of the big picture is one of my strengths. The challenge I face is breaking it down to first steps, creating a plan, and then taking action. Don't get me wrong, I am a person of action. I have an idea, and then I get to work. While this is actually a good thing most of the time, the risk is that it can lead to burnout. If planning and organizing are difficult for you, you may want to surround yourself with people who have that strength. These are likely the S or C personality styles in the DISC profile. To get your

DISC profile, visit http://www.movedbypurpose.
net/shop/disc-personality-profile-2/

Outlines and mind maps help to organize
thoughts. Breaking down my ideas and planning out
the process I should use are not actually my strength.
It's ironic how I'm a coach who helps people break
down their goals and create action plans. I'm really
good at doing it for others, but have a challenge being
objective with my own goals. This is why I have no
shame in hiring coaches and working with others who
can remain objective and see things I just don't see for
myself. This is exactly what successful people do for any
area where they are not strong: they seek wise counsel.

The simplest ideas have created breakthrough
results when I work with my coaches. The same has
happened for my own clients working with me. One
of the best pieces of advice that I received was from
my then-boyfriend (now husband). He told me to
create an outline for every idea that I have. This helped
me write down my ideas in a very structured and
organized manner. I had never bothered writing an
outline before, because I thought it just wasted time.

Quite the contrary—outlines *save* so much time! I write an outline for just about everything now.

- My daily to-do list is written in outline form and numbered according to priority.

- My tasks written to my team members are written in outline form. This helps them catch all the details and ensures that each task is done correctly.

- My book was written in an outline. Confession: I started this book with no outline. Then I confused myself with what was already written and where. An outline eliminated that confusion quickly!

- All of my programs, trainings, courses, and groups are written in outlines.

- I even outline my email and phone pitches. This makes sure they are clear, concise, and easy to follow.

Prioritize the Essential. The noise of every little thing can make it loud and crowded inside our heads.

Delegate the rest. Learning how to delegate is extremely important. If there's enough room in the budget, hiring a personal assistant to go grocery shopping, do the laundry, mow the lawn, or do other tasks can free up *so much* time and energy. The more tasks we can get off of our plates, the better off we are.

The first lesson I learned when I was building my business around my day job was the importance of outsourcing tasks. Anything that did not make me money or build a valuable relationship was delegated. That included social-media management, email management, website management, publishing my podcast and blogs, and so on. I would write the content, but someone else did the photos, SEO, taglines, and links.

Disappointment Over Interim or Even Global Failures

If our Great Work fails and totally bites the dust, we may be tempted to blame all manner of people around us, and some of us have a glorious go at trying to blame God for our woes, too (that one started with Adam in the Garden of Eden: "The woman that *you* gave me . . ."). My mentors and I certainly have a lot of experience at doing this ourselves, so we know this game very well.

But the failure of a "great idea" can still be our path to a more meaningful triumph. Remember that the main questions we asked ourselves have very little to do with satisfying our own egos and pocketbooks, but are wider in scope and concern themselves with the execution of God's will.

Our failure may be telling us that we were going off the rails from the start. It might mean that we are simply not paying attention to what needful thing actually *was* accomplished. It could be a call to make sure that in our next efforts we think and pray *first* about whether we're doing something for the Lord's sake or just for our own. This can show us how to listen to counsel more effectively and honestly and how to stop fooling ourselves.

We find out these answers the same way as we have been talking about: prayer, counsel, honesty, and reflection. Are you getting the idea about how plainly universal this solution can be?

Breaking Bad Habits

This is probably more familiar territory for some of us. In fact, if you have ever had a friend check you on a bad habit you're trying to break, by telling you when you're doing it again, this is the essence of the kind of counsel that we have been talking about. You have been honest and humble enough with this friend to let them know you know you're doing badly. And you're trusting yourself to their direction by letting them call you out on your misbehavior.

Welcome to the company of the best—this is a very ancient technique that makes bad people into good people, and even into saints.

Overcoming Distraction

Distraction is a subset of "bad habits," if we are really honest about this. Here, again, we have to check our 21st century ideas and excuses at the door. No, the big problem is not some label the psychologist gave us. It is that we are in a cultivated bad habit of not paying attention to what is in front of us.

How does anyone break a bad habit? Effort and practice. But it is rare that we will change a bad habit without letting someone know we are striving to do so. It is difficult work to change a pattern of behavior, but it can be done with steady, unflinching effort. Think here of how Nehemiah dealt with the threats from the enemies of Israel. He continued his work with his people but set up a guard where half of the people worked and half watched, and all worked with their battle gear strapped on and at the ready.

When we are going through the middle of a change, this image is helpful—we get the job done by constant vigilance and remaining prepared at all times. If we relax too much, more often than not the bad habit kicks in with all its force and we have to start over at changing. It is easier on us to practice simple, calm vigilance.

And calm vigilance is the practice of being undistracted.

change your
MINDSET

Mindsets are extremely powerful. Another word for "mindset" is "stronghold." A mindset can be positive or negative. A controversial statement or belief that I have is that most poverty in the developed world is caused by a mindset. As a social worker, my client base consisted of people living in poverty. I saw destructive, limiting, small, and negative thinking hold people down and keep them from breaking free from the oppressive, vicious cycle of poverty. Some people in the world are truly oppressed by a corrupt government or some other force that holds them in the dire situation they are in. But for most of us in the "First World," living in poverty is caused by a mindset.

Prosperity and abundance are also mindsets. Some people have the core belief that their success raises up everyone else. Their increase means more increase and gain for others. Someone else who offers a similar product or service means another person to partner with and collaborate with, not compete with. These people often live with plenty and give generously.

Our thought patterns have been with us for a while. It's important to keep the door closed to the familiar negative voice and to meditate on the Truth. We must remind ourselves that what we really have is good. We call the lies what they are—lies—and shoo them away.

Here are seven steps to call out the lies:

1. Identify a negative feeling. Are you agitated? Anxious? Worried? Those are sidekicks of fear.

2. Ask God to help you learn when this fear first appeared in your life.

3. If memories come up, repent or turn away from the lies you believed.

4. Forgive all involved in this event.

5. Release them to God. Even if you are angry with God, release the offense, anger, and hurt to Him.

6. Ask God what He has in exchange.

7. Receive it.

A Word About "Diagnoses" and Mentorship

Would you believe that there are very few psychologists in Russia? It is true. And most Russian people are extremely pragmatic and centered in terms of what they have to do. They are disciplined. It is really difficult to throw a Russian person off the discipline with which they live their life. This is the result of a very ancient way of life that started at least 1,000 years ago and continued right through the Soviet era until now. The Russians are beginning to struggle with some of the same problems in their grade schools that the Americans now face, because the Russians have tried to adopt the Western model of education and culture.

Oops.

They may be about 35 years behind us in terms of the level to which they have adopted our lifestyle, but they are also about 35 years behind us in terms of diagnoses of mental illness and incapacitation. Think there might be a connection?

Well, the connection is largely based on this matter of trusting counsel. Even though the Soviet period deliberately eschewed God and any manner of religious reality, the cultural element of humility did not change much. Kids still knew to do as they were told, and they knew to trust the direction they were given. Adults were not afflicted with rugged individualism and even to this day, many Russian adults display an amazing amount of humility regarding what others say to them. It's not all the time, and not 100%, but it is enough to have developed an emotionally and psychologically healthy and strong nation.

Among the religious Russians, we see even more serenity of purpose. Many Russian people follow the practice of going to an elder in the church, called a *staretz*, for deep counsel and advice. Some Russians travel hundreds or even thousands of miles to meet with the staretz to seek his or her counsel. They trust this counsel as the word of God for them personally.

This is nothing new; it is a continuation of a tradition that predates Christianity, but that is central to it.

American flavors of the Christian faith have largely rejected this principle, but it is still alive and well in many parts of the world, and where it exists, the people have more stability and serenity.

It is not necessary to seek holy men thousands of miles away to find this counsel. We often fantasize about meeting the wise old man on the mountaintop and getting the advice that fixes everything, but that is not how it works.

We *do* seek wise people, but often the times spent talking to them are incremental rather than revolutionary in how they affect our lives. Sometimes our parents or grandparents are great sources of wisdom. Sometimes it is a person who has experienced success in our chosen area of work. Sometimes it is someone completely unknown to us, like a person we meet in the grocery store or at the post office. If we are praying for God to show his will to us, He will do so, and we simply have to be ready to hear and act on it.

Nehemiah prayed in this way. He had no idea *how* God would answer his prayer, or even *if* He would in any known way at all. But he made himself ready to act when the chance came, and when it did, he prayed again and stepped forward in faith to do what he needed to do.

messy middle
SURVIVED

Success Stories

Melissa AuClair, thecreativeseason.com helps small business owners streamline their business to what is most important. Here's what she has to say about her Messy Middle.

> It has been about six years since I started the journey of finding my vision. About 18 months ago, I began to grasp a dream and put words to that vision. It hasn't all come to pass, but the difference between me today and me in 2006 is that I know my strengths, I know where I want to go, and who I want to impact. This knowledge makes all the difference.

To get there, I went through a lot of emotions! Frustration and tears as many things didn't work out. Most people in my life didn't understand my internal struggle and were content in their regular jobs. *Like many people, I was on my own trying to navigate in an ocean I didn't have the map to!*

On the other side of frustration is the incredible amount of good things I've learned and the people I've met. I went through a couple of years of learning the skill of copywriting. While I don't work as a copywriter, the skill helps me in my writing, blogging, and web content. I've learned so many interesting things and read hundreds of books. I've met people at conferences and through the web that I never would have met otherwise.

Finally, even though the journey has taken a long time, I've grown in ways I never would have imagined if the journey had been easy. Fears have been overcome, insecurities are being conquered, and I've developed an intense desire to help others who are experiencing similar situations.

Along the way, I learned that mainstream media—offline and online—would have us believe success is fairly easy and for those who are special in some way. Even magazines like Entrepreneur, Fast Company, and Inc. (which I love) highlight the immense success of people who are young and have achieved huge milestones. These stories often make the news because they are pretty radical—they're newsworthy.

But "success," however you define it, takes a lot of work and time and effort, and many times it's not all that glamorous.

Sarah Blakley (founder of Spanx) went through many years of super hard work before she landed on *Forbes* as the first self-made female billionaire. She says,

Finding our passion and creating work that matches that AND pays the bills is challenging. It's not unlike growing a garden. Some of the seeds don't make it. There are weeds. Birds come and grab fruit. A dry season can wipe out weak plants. Rain storms come. (Ironically, the storms often help produce the strongest crops).

Some people will find success quickly. I'm not one of them. Most people I talk to are like me, working day in and day out to create a life that reflects their passions and values. It's okay.

The only thing that isn't okay is to put it off because of fear and anxiety! The time to start is now.

I've also learned I need to enjoy the process and find joy in the small accomplishments. I try to remember the verse, "Don't despise the day of small beginnings." Building the foundation for meaningful work may not be glamorous, but it's essential.

Believe that your desires and passions are there for a reason. Don't be afraid of a time when it seems nothing is happening while you are working. More is happening than you can tell—we often can't see our own initial growth. Find a group of people who will support you and give you tough love; this has made all the difference for me.

Believe that you are here for a unique purpose and your time is now. So many people have lost their belief in the value of their dreams and desires. Don't give up. Don't ever give up.

And don't compare. It's the worst thing to do with the most unhelpful results. We all have our own journeys. We go at different paces. As Jo Packham, one of the creative women I admire, says, "There is room for everyone at the table." There really is. *With hard work, perseverance, and developing your skills, you will find your place at the table.*

Kent Julian is a successful entrepreneur and an exemplary human being. He is a motivational speaker today. As a child, no one would have ever thought that speaking was his call/purpose in life.

Here is his story:

I faced considerable challenges growing up. For instance, I had a significant speech impediment as a child and could not pronounce the sounds associated with the letters "*f, g, j, k, l, r, s, v, z, ch, sh, th,* and related consonant blends." Additionally, by the time I reached third grade, my teacher called my parents in for a private conference to ask them how I passed the previous grades without being able to read. These academic struggles continued to follow me throughout school, so much so that when I graduated high school, my SAT scores were so low I had to take Developmental Studies before being accepted into college on probation.

But academics were not the only challenges I faced. When I entered middle school, I was an "at-risk" teen with zero self-confidence. I was making poor friendship choices and even poorer life choices. One bad step led to another and another and another until finally I experienced an event that changed the course of my life. It wasn't a positive experience. It was a colossal mistake. The details aren't necessary, just know *it was major!* But my positive response to this event, which I learned from an exceptional educator and advisor, changed the course of my life and caused me to become fully engaged in taking 100 percent responsibility for my life.

Kent's story is one that I often refer back to when I feel that my efforts are not yielding the results I was hoping for. It took him three years of hard work to generate $60,000 in his business. Now, he is making half a million and counting per year.

The beauty is that no two journeys are the same. Just like we each have our own unique purpose or destiny, our pathways to get there are different. No two will be exactly alike.

COMMUNITY

In addition to educating ourselves and keeping our emotions from hijacking the journey, we need community. We need a group of safe people we trust to give honest feedback, believe in us, and hold us accountable. They will challenge destructive, limiting beliefs to bring us higher. It's imperative to choose that community carefully. It's not helpful to have a bunch of other people who are lost. At least one person needs to have clarity. It's great to have a group of likeminded people and to know you are not alone, but there needs to be an expert guide, coach, mentor, or teacher to help lead the community. Proven groups or models that demonstrate the success and power of this are organizations such as AA. The common theme in that group is alcohol—members are either currently battling it or have successfully conquered it. Weight Watchers is another example of this model, with accountability through weekly weigh-ins. The members work toward the same goal: losing weight and creating a healthy lifestyle (community) and are led by a teacher (expert) who guides the discussions.

Group coaching has the same advantages of organizations like that. Group coaching programs are my favorite form of coaching. I make sure to have members who need clarity and guidance to get where they want to go. The members have a connection with each other because they no longer feel alone and overwhelmed. My role is to guide, redirect, ask probing questions, and cheer them on to success. I also give the necessary individualized attention to the members by including one-on-one coaching sessions. It's an extremely powerful model.

Mastermind groups are another way to build community and support for our Great Work. The best mastermind groups usually have a fee associated with them. This ensures that every member is committed to the group. If there is no investment, it's unlikely for everyone to really show up and contribute. That's just human psychology: we value things we spend our own money on more than we value things that are free or paid for by someone else.

Habits are powerful things that people do with little to no thought. They are developed by consistent behavior. It is important to have awareness of what we are doing and saying. We all have habits. Some people are more structured and organized; others go with the flow. Some are more prone to getting caught in a Messy Middle than others are, but now we know how to get through it.

CONCLUSION

It would seem that the chief cause of our Messy Middle is an over-reliance on no one but ourselves, and expecting a worthy work to go smoothly from start to success. We have even held God captive to our own wishes rather than truly seeking His will about our lives, and the result is obvious. The needed power to sustain any steady track just does not exist with us.

We have offered you, the reader, some very clear instructions, based on very ancient principles. Although not all of those principles have been lost in our culture, the really important ones have been supplanted with rugged individualism and misled expectations. The result for many of us has been internal mental and emotional chaos, as well as an inability to achieve or succeed. Many people want instant results and don't want to wait for anything. Many of us feel that if we work hard, we should be rewarded—immediately. We have been doing it *by* ourselves alone and *for* ourselves alone, without appropriate expectations and patience, and the results are not that good.

We have also looked at what a believer in ancient times did, pointed out the stark differences between his approach to accomplishment and ours, and pointed the way we may follow to resume living as we really were made to—to live in humble obedience and reliance upon the grace of God.

Under His grace, there may be quite a roller-coaster ride, but *there is no need for the emotional turmoil, the Messy Middle.* There is only the journey. We invite you to experience this "new" old way of life, and to come to truly know what it is like to have God's blessings in abundance.

If we really want God to get the glory, we must get out of the way and submit to His way. His way will often take much longer than we prefer, and will be far more work than we imagined. However, do not forget that God is just. The reward will exceed anything you could possibly hope for, imagine, or even think to ask for (Ephesians 3:20).

This season may feel like it has dragged out and stolen years from your life, but remember that Nehemiah did the unthinkable in just 52 days. Your life will be changed. All the preparation, all the difficulty, all the pain and suffering will have played a necessary role in how you fulfill your purpose. Don't try to get out of it early. In due season, that bountiful harvest will come if you do not give up, so persevere and persist, my friend. What *great joy* awaits the person who endures. What an exquisitely beautiful relationship that person has developed with their creator. That person gets to really and truly know God. I don't know how many people really know God as the Great I AM, the One who is close to the brokenhearted, who heals the sick and raises the dead to life, but I know they are far better off for knowing Him.

He is our Jehovah Rapha, Our Great Physician.
He is our Jehovah Tsidkenu, The Lord our Righteousness.
He is our Jehovah Jireh, Our Great Provider.
He is our Jehovah Nissi, Our Great Banner.
He is our Jehovah Raah, Our Great Shepherd.
He is our Jehovah Shammah, The One who is There.
He is Jehovah Shalom, Our Great Peace.
He is Jehovah Sabaoth, The Lord of Hosts.

It is His will to heal, and He loves us more than we can ever know. It doesn't mean we always get what we desire, and it certainly doesn't mean we get it when we want it. But the journey is worth every step.

I often mention in my podcast that doing something is better than doing nothing. Here I'll take it further: Doing something with the knowledge that you're doing the right thing and that you have the determination to see it through and trust the process is best.

Wishing you God's best,

Stephanie O'Brien-Martin

thank
YOU'S

Thank you to everyone involved with making my dream of writing this book a reality. Chris Martin, this book would have never happened without your constant support through my messy middle. Dan Miller, Thank you for teaching me to dream big and to believe in the call on my life. Diamond Girls, thank you for your constant prayers to lift me up in my weary moments. Finally, thank you to Morgan James Publishing specifically, Karen Anderson, for taking the time to listen to the concept of this book and believing in its message to present it to the board at Morgan James. To Gayle West, author relations manager thank you for your patience and professionalism with all of my questions through the publishing process.

about the
AUTHOR

Stephanie O'Brien-Martin, founder and creator of MovedbyPurpose.net, knows from experience that finding and living your purpose can change your career, your happiness, and your life.

As a renowned and acclaimed life coach specializing in "purpose coaching", Stephanie is in high demand to share her proven systems for helping individuals find and follow their purpose as well as create meaningful work. Don't try to discover your life's calling on your own, when Stephanie can guide you down the path to "finding your wings".

Stephanie has the unique ability to connect with individuals, the insight to see where they're struggling, highlight their strengths and realign their life with their passions that lead to purpose. Drawing on her experience as a social worker, and as a speaker and small group leader in various non-denominational churches in the Greater Detroit area she has an unrelenting passion to align individuals with their higher calling and find a way to craft their life around their purpose, or as she says, "what makes your soul sing". A top student of Dan Miller, New York Times Bestselling Author of '48 Days to the Work You Love', Stephanie is also a certified Master Life Coach with a strong mix of corporate and in-the-field experience. Since beginning her radical journey, she has also been the top listened to podcast on the Relaunch Show, with over 1 million downloads worldwide, and has been featured on Entrepreneur On Fire in 2015, the number one business podcast on iTunes.